A TALKING POINTS BOOK BY
VAUGHAN ROBERTS

?

TRANSGENDER

Transgender
© Vaughan Roberts/The Good Book Company, 2016

Published by
The Good Book Company
Tel (UK): 0333 123 0880
Tel (North America): (1) 866 244 2165
International: +44 (0) 208 942 0880
Email (UK): info@thegoodbook.co.uk
Email (North America): info@thegoodbook.com

Websites
UK & Europe: www.thegoodbook.co.uk
North America: www.thegoodbook.com
Australia: www.thegoodbook.com.au
New Zealand: www.thegoodbook.co.nz

Unless otherwise indicated, Scripture quotations are from the The
Holy Bible, New International Version, NIV Copyright © 1973, 1978,
1984, 2011 by Biblica, Inc.

ISBN: 9781784981952

Printed in the UK by CPI

Design by André Parker

CONTENTS

Introduction: Talking Points   7

    1. Transgender   13
    2. The iWorld   25
    3. Creation   35
    4. Fall   45
    5. Rescue   55
    6. Wisdom   65

Further reading   75
Acknowledgements   76

INTRODUCTION

TALKING POINTS

The world is changing. Fast.

And not just politics, technology and communication, but our whole culture, morality and attitudes. Christians living in Western culture have enjoyed the benefit of being in a world which largely shared our assumptions about what is fundamentally right and wrong. We can no longer assume that this is the case.

In two short generations we have moved to a widespread adoption of liberal values, many of which are in conflict with the teaching of the Bible. Increasingly, believers are finding themselves to be the misunderstood minority, and feeling at odds with where the world seems to be heading.

Let's not deny it: some of this has been good. Christians have often failed to discern the difference between our own cultural values, and those that are demanded by Scripture. We are as prone to bigotry as others. We have much to repent of in our attitudes towards the freedom and role of women in society, and in our lack of compassion and understanding towards, for example, those who have wrestled with same-sex attraction.

But now, again, we find ourselves in unfamiliar territory and ill-equipped to deal with it. Sometimes it's easier to protest and rage against the tide of history than to go back to our Bibles and think carefully about what God is saying—holding up society's views, and our own, to the truth-revealing mirror that is God's word.

At our best, we Christians have been in the forefront of social reform. Think of the great nineteenth-century reformers of the slave trade, prisons and poverty: William Wilberforce, Elizabeth Fry and Lord Shaftesbury. But now we find ourselves on the back foot, unable to articulate a clear response to a pressing question of our day. And even when we have understood God's mind on a particular issue, we have struggled to apply it compassionately in our speech and in our relationships.

This short series of books is an attempt to help ordinary Christians start to think constructively about a range of issues—moral, ethical and cultural—that run against the grain for those who name Christ as Lord. They are an attempt to stimulate believers to start talking with each other as we search the Scriptures together. Their aim is to help us think biblically, constructively and compassionately, and not to feel intimidated when we are challenged or questioned, or, perhaps worse, remain silent.

WHAT THIS BOOK IS NOT...
In such a short book, we cannot hope to answer all the questions you may have about how to think on this issue. Nor can we address the many practical challenges you may be facing with family or friends, or personally.

Nor does it present a thorough treatment of all the Bible has to say on these questions. If that is what you are hungry for, there will be other, longer, and perhaps more technical books that will help you dig deeper.

WHAT THIS BOOK IS...
Rather, our aim is to give you an accessible introduction to the many questions that surround the transgender issue, as we hold our questions up to the big story of the Bible: the story of creation, fall, redemption and eternity.

But we also hope that it takes us all beyond the issue—to a genuine compassion and love for those who are caught up in some way with these questions. They may be questions that are deeply personal to you. They may be questions that are thrown at you in a proud, assertive and hostile way. Or they may be questions that are real because they affect a close family member or friend. Whatever your situation, we hope this book will be a first step towards understanding the landscape, and an encouragement to know and share the love and hope we have in Christ.

Tim Thornborough
Series Editor
August 2016

transgender

[trans-**jen**-der, tranz-]

adjective, also, **transgendered**
1. noting or relating to a person whose gender identity does not correspond to that person's biological sex assigned at birth.
2. noting or relating to a person who does not conform to societal gender norms or roles.

noun
a person who is **transgender**.

[Source: dictionary.com]

There's a gender in your brain and a gender in your body. For 99% of people, those things are in alignment. For transgender people, they're mismatched. That's all it is. It's not complicated, it's not a neurosis. It's a mix-up. It's a birth defect, like a cleft palate.
**Chaz Bono,
Transgender activist and entertainer**

34% of trans people attempt suicide. 64% are bullied. 73% of trans people are harassed in public. 21% of trans people avoid going out in public due to fear.
Transgender Remembrance Day poster

"Some men are born in their bodies, others have to fight for it."
Transgender slogan

We're human beings, and this is a human life. This is reality for us, and all we ask for is acceptance and validation for what we say that we are. It's a basic human right.
Andreja Pejic, Transgender model

So God created mankind in his own image, in the image of God he created them; male and female he created them.
Genesis 1 v 27

TRANSGENDER

CHAPTER ONE

There's been huge cultural change in the last few decades. Same-sex marriage would have been unthinkable 20 or 30 years ago. Now it's almost universally accepted in the Western world. And then suddenly the transgender issue is the next big social, ethical and cultural question that has come to dominate the headlines.

Hardly a week goes by, it seems, without there being some kind of transgender story in the news—and the stories will keep on coming. There has been the transitioning of Bruce, now Caitlin, Jenner, the former decathlon world-record holder. Then we've had the debates over the rights and wrongs of which public bathrooms (restrooms) to use, which prison transgender people should be sent to, whether transgender people can serve in the military, and what to put on passports. There have been a number of television documentaries, including one by Louis Theroux on transgender children. And on the big screen *The Danish Girl* is a dramatised account of the artist Lili Elbe—one of the first people known to have undergone sex-change surgery.

How should Christians respond to all this—not just in the media and wider culture but, closer to home, in our communities, families and churches? How should we relate to someone who is transitioning gender or has already transitioned? And what if the sense of not fitting with the sex of one's birth is a deeply personal one for us? How should we respond?

We need to begin by remembering that we are not simply talking about "issues" here, but people: precious individuals, each created and loved by God. Most of them don't have a strong political agenda or any desire to fight in a "culture war"; they are simply trying to cope with feelings that may well cause them great distress. Too often they are being damaged in the crossfire of what can become a very heated debate. As will become clear later, I do think Christians should contribute to that public discussion, but it's vitally important that we do so with great sensitivity and compassion. Let's never forget those who are most deeply affected by this subject and let's ensure that we try to understand what they are experiencing.

WHAT IS TRANSGENDER?

When a child is born, it's likely that the first thing anyone will say is, "It's a boy" or "It's a girl". Assigning someone's sex has traditionally been based on biology—their chromosomes and anatomy. But for some people, their sense of gender—their inner feelings of being male, female, or both—doesn't always match that sex.

Many people have assumptions about what it means to be transgender but, fundamentally, it isn't about surgery or how someone dresses. It's about how they feel inside. It's not the same as sexuality or sexual orientation. People often confuse transgender and homosexuality, perhaps because the two are included together in the LGBT grouping (Lesbian, Gay, Bisexual, Transgender). But those who identify as transgender may consider themselves heterosexual, homosexual or bisexual (or, perhaps, pansexual, polysexual, or asexual), just as the rest of the population might.

And transgender is not the same as intersex (the I in LGBTI). Intersex is a physical condition affecting a very small percentage of people whose chromosomes, genitals or gonads do not allow them to be distinctively identified as male or female at birth. The great majority of them do not identify as transgender, but rather as male or female. By contrast, transgender is to do with how people think or feel. They are born either male or female, but their feelings about their gender don't fit with their sex.

MANY PEOPLE: MANY EXPRESSIONS

Transgender is an umbrella term that covers a wide range of experiences. Each person's story is unique and their journey intensely personal. Some say they are the opposite gender to what they were assigned at birth. Some feel they are both male and female. Still others don't identify as either gender.

There will be differences in the nature and intensity of the feelings people have. So, for some, their questions may be just in the background and then come more to the foreground at certain times, or at a particular point in life.

For others, there may be significant confusion during childhood which then disappears. In fact the majority of children who experience these strong feelings find that they disappear completely during adolescence.[1]

But for others, there is a prolonged sense of disharmony within them that causes great distress. Profes-

---

1 When children who reported transgender feelings were tracked without medical or surgical treatment at both Vanderbilt University and London's Portman Clinic, 70%-80% of them spontaneously lost those feelings. Dr Paul McHugh, *Wall Street Journal,* June 12, 2014

sionals call this "gender dysphoria". These individuals frequently speak about feeling they are trapped in the wrong body, and will often testify that these thoughts go right back to very early childhood, maybe the age of 5 or 6. Many also describe a sense of profound isolation in the following years and of difficulty sharing how they feel with others because of fear they will be misunderstood or rejected.

There are differences in experience, and there are also differences in how these feelings are expressed and whether or not they are acted on outwardly. Some live within the norms of their birth sex. Others cross-dress occasionally—whether in private only or also in public. Some ask people to change the pronouns they use to identify them. (They may choose "he", "she", "they", or even "ze"). Some undergo hormone therapy and sex reassignment surgery.

Gender dysphoria is defined as a "marked incongruence between one's experienced/expressed gender and assigned gender, of at least 6 months' duration",[2] which causes significant distress. Studies suggest that between 1 in 10,000 and 1 in 13,000 males and between 1 in 20,000 and 1 in 34,000

---

2 American Psychiatric Association, *Diagnostic and Statistical Manual of Mental Disorders, 5th edition* (Washington DC: American Psychiatric Publishing, 2013) p. 452

females have this condition.[3] Many more people report some sense of incongruence, but not to the extent that they are diagnosed as having gender dysphoria—perhaps between 1 in 215 and 1 in 300 people.[4]

There is no agreement on what causes gender dysphoria. Some argue that nature makes the most significant contribution. They promote, for example, the brain-sex theory, according to which transgender people have a male-type brain in a female body, or vice versa. The evidence for this view is far from conclusive.[5] Others believe that nurture—psychological environment in childhood—is the dominant factor. After a thorough survey of the arguments on both sides, one author honestly admits: "We don't know what causes gender dysphoria".[6] Given the breadth of the transgender experience, it seems likely that the

---

3 Mark A. Yarhouse, *Understanding Gender Dysphoria* (Downers Grove IL: IVP 2015), p. 92

4 Yarhouse, p. 92

5 After a thorough survey of the evidence Lawrence Mayer and Paul McHugh comment: "All interpretations, usually in popular outlets, claiming or suggesting that a statistically significant difference between the brains of people who are transgender and those who are not is the cause of being transgender or not … are unwarranted." Lawrence H. Mayer, Paul R. McHugh, *Sexuality and Gender,* The New Atlantis, Number 50, Fall 2016.

6 Yarhouse, p. 79

contributing factors vary from person to person and may include elements of both nature and nurture. In all the uncertainty, however, one thing is clear: those who experience gender dysphoria certainly do not simply choose to do so.

OUR CHRISTIAN RESPONSE

There are two common responses to this issue: an unquestioning "Yuk!" and an unquestioning "Yes!" In previous years, those who decided to cross-dress in public would have been received by most people with a "Yuk!" response.

"Yuk, it's disgusting!" Not thought through—just an emotional response.

But now the response of many, especially younger people, would just be of unquestioning affirmation.

"That's good—it's great to be yourself!" Not thought through—just an emotional response.

Christians should avoid both these reactions. Rather than turning away from people in disgust with a "Yuk!", we need to remember that they are made in God's image and deeply loved by him. We should share his compassion for them in their pain and confusion.

Most of us can only begin to imagine the distress that might be associated with gender dysphoria. Certainly no one ends up in an operating theatre for a radically invasive surgical procedure having taken the decision lightly. We have to recognise that there must be a huge amount of prolonged distress and struggle behind that decision. So it's vital that we Christians take care never to think or talk of those who struggle in this way with any kind of disrespect. We must speak with compassion and affirm the dignity of every human being. We are all made in the image of God.

One important way we can do this is to understand more clearly what it is that they are going through. It is also important not to speak in a manner that they find hurtful or degrading. For that reason I have chosen to use the definitions from the Stonewall website for the glossary of terms on pages 21-24. Stonewall is an LGBT rights organisation.

As Christians, we shouldn't let our responses be governed by our gut reactions, whether positive or negative, but by God's word. Chapters 3 to 5 will help us understand what the Bible has to say on our subject. It certainly demands that we respond to all human suffering with compassion, but it also gives us convictions which sometimes clash with the way many people think today, so that we can't just say "Yes!" to all that the world affirms.

But before we look at what the Bible says, in our next chapter we will think a bit more about our culture, which has been changing so rapidly. How is it that an unquestioning "Yuk!" has been replaced, for very many people at least, with an unquestioning "Yes!"? We will see that this is just one symptom of a much broader cultural shift.

UNDERSTANDING TRANSGENDER LANGUAGE

These definitions come from the Stonewall website. I have retained the language they use, although I am uncomfortable with references to "sex assigned at birth". Our sex is not simply "assigned", but is given to us by God.

Cisgender or Cis. Someone whose gender identity is the same as the sex they were assigned at birth. "Non-trans" is also used by some people.

Gender dysphoria. Used to describe when a person experiences discomfort or distress because there is a mis-match between their sex assigned at birth and their gender identity. This is also the clinical diagnosis for someone who doesn't feel comfortable with the gender they were assigned at birth.

Gender identity. A person's internal sense of their own gender, whether male, female or something else (see "non-binary" below).

Gender reassignment. Another way of describing a person's transition. To undergo gender reassignment usually means to undergo some sort of medical intervention, but it can also mean changing names, pronouns, dressing differently and living in their self-identified gender. Gender reassignment is a characteristic that is protected by the Equality Act 2010.

Intersex. A term used to describe a person who may have the biological attributes of both sexes or whose biological attributes do not fit with societal assumptions about what constitutes male or female. Intersex people can identify as male, female, or non-binary.

Non-binary. An umbrella term for a person who does not identify as male or female.

Queer. In the past a derogatory term for LGBT individuals. The term has now been reclaimed by LGBT young people in particular who don't identify with traditional categories around gender identity and sexual orientation but is still viewed as derogatory by some.

Trans/Transgender. An umbrella term to describe people whose gender is not the same as, or does not sit comfortably with, the sex they were assigned at birth. Trans people may describe themselves using one or more of a wide variety of terms, including (but not limited to) transgender, cross-dresser, non-binary, genderqueer (GQ).

Transgender man. A term used to describe someone who is assigned female at birth but identifies and lives as a man. This may be shortened to trans man, or FTM, an abbreviation for female-to-male.

Transgender woman. A term used to describe someone who is assigned male at birth but identifies and lives as a woman. This may be shortened to trans woman, or MTF, an abbreviation for male-to-female.

Transitioning. The steps a trans person may take to live in the gender with which they identify. Each person's transition will involve different things. For some this involves medical intervention, such as hormone therapy and surgeries, but not all trans people want or are able to have this. Transitioning also might involve things such as telling friends and family, dressing differently and changing official documents.

Transexual. This was used in the past as a more medical term (similarly to homosexual) to refer to someone who transitioned to live in the "opposite" gender to the one assigned at birth. This term is still used by some although many people prefer the term trans or transgender.

[Source: www.stonewall.org.uk/help-advice/
glossary-terms]

THE iWORLD

CHAPTER TWO

A significant part of Steve Jobs' success was his genius at marketing. He wasn't just able to produce great products; he also had an acute understanding of the spirit of the age, which enabled him to create a brand that appealed to our culture's deepest longings. The names of his Apple products—the iMac, the iPod, the iPhone, and the iPad—are striking. Jobs knew that we live in the iWorld,[7] in which everything revolves around the individual.

The roots of the profound individualism that marks our culture go back to the period of the Enlightenment 300 years ago, when intellectuals began to assert the primacy of human reason over

---

7 This term comes from Dale Kuehne's excellent book *Sex and the iWorld* (Grand Rapids Mich.: Baker Academic 2009)

divine revelation. Most people have never read the works of philosophers like Voltaire and Rousseau, but their influence has gradually trickled down into our whole society so that it affects us all.

The Enlightenment began with great confidence that reason could lead us to the truth, but that optimism gradually disappeared. Even the greatest human thinkers can't agree on fundamental issues. And so, having rejected revelation and lacking confidence in reason, our culture has now largely rejected the concept of objective truth, at least when it comes to big issues, such as meaning and morality.

So where does this leave us? With ourselves as individuals. If we think that truth is subjective, then we certainly won't let any external authority tell us what to think or how to behave—whether it's the government, a religion or our family. It's up to us to draw our own conclusions and live our own lives. As the boys from Boyzone put it in one of their songs:

> *No matter what they tell you;*
> *no matter what they say;*
> *no matter what they teach you;*
> *what you believe is true.*

All this explains why autonomy is so highly valued today. The iWorld teaches me to resent any challenge to my individualism. As the English philosopher

John Stuart Mill, the founding father of modern Western liberalism, wrote:

> *Over himself, over his own body and mind, the individual is sovereign.*[8]

I'm free! Free to think what I want and live as I like. Free to be me.

That leads us to the next highly prized value today: authenticity. Above all else, we must be true to ourselves. Jonathan Grant has expressed it well:

> *Modern authenticity encourages us to create our own beliefs and morality, the only rule being that they must resonate with who we feel we really are. The worst thing we can do is to conform to some moral code that is imposed on us from outside—by society, our parents, the church, or whoever else. It is deemed to be self-evident that any such imposition would undermine our unique identity ... The authentic self believes that personal meaning must be found within ourselves or must resonate with our one-of-a-kind personality.*[9]

---

8 John Stuart Mill, *On Liberty*, ed. Elizabeth Rapaport (Indianapolis: Hackett 1979), p. 9

9 Jonathan Grant, *Divine Sex* (Grand Rapids MI: Brazos Press 2015), p. 30

Grant has commented that "this culture of expressive individualism has become the moral wallpaper of the modern world."[10] Over the last few decades the primacy of self-expression has become an unquestioned assumption of many. No one has the right to question or challenge how each individual chooses to define themselves.

It should be obvious by now how these changes in our cultural values have impacted the way that many view gender. If we are free to define our own identity without being bound by the old conventions, then that will include the outdated, constricting, binary, male-or-female understanding of gender. Here is how American feminist writer Camille Paglia puts it:

> *I consider myself neither gay nor straight, neither male nor female, neither human being nor animal.*

Judith Lorber, a radical feminist, writes that she longs for the day when gender distinctives have effectively disappeared:

> *When we no longer ask "boy or girl?"' in order to start gendering an infant, when the information is as irrelevant as the colour of a child's eyes ... only then will men and women be socially interchangeable and really equal. And*

---

10 Grant, p. 34

when that happens there will no longer be any need for gender at all.[11]

Change is already happening quickly. Facebook recently started allowing users to customise their gender: "male", "female" or "other". The "other" category listed 71 options, including bi-gender, transgender, androgynous and trans-sexual. An employee of Facebook at the time said, "We want to help users to be their *true, authentic selves*". But things have moved on so quickly that Facebook's "other" category has now been changed to "custom", with a blank field allowing users to opt for any gender label of their choosing.

One slogan puts it like this: "Anatomy isn't destiny". In other words, your anatomy needn't determine your gender. And developments in medicine and surgery mean that your anatomy needn't determine your sex. You're free—even from nature. Not even our bodies should be allowed to restrict us in our self-definition.

Where will all this end? There was discomfort in the media when Rachel Dolezal, a civil-rights activist, was accused by her parents of falsely claiming to be black, when she was in fact white.

---

11 Quoted in *Are we all "omnigender" now?* by Sharon James at www.affinity.org.uk

She responded by insisting that she still "identified as black". The case of a young Norwegian woman was also widely reported. Claiming to have the sensory powers of a cat, she said she had been born "in the wrong species".[12]

Although most people would feel that these self-identifications have gone too far, there is still an uneasiness about challenging any individual's chosen self-expression. There's a deeply rooted conviction that everyone is free to define themselves as they wish, and no one has the right to question that self-definition. That explains why our culture's knee-jerk reaction to those identifying as transgender has changed from an unquestioning *"Yuk!"* to an unquestioning "Yes!" That shift has been rapid in recent years.

One significant sign of the change in public attitudes is seen in the language that is used. The 1994 edition of the *US Diagnostic and Statistical Manual of Mental Disorders* referred to cross-gender identification as "gender identity disorder". The next edition in 2013 describes the same phenomenon as "gender dysphoria",[13] so that the emphasis is not on

---

12 Quoted in Glynn Harrison, *A Better Story: God, Sex and Human Flourishing,* (London: IVP, forthcoming publication).

13 Christian Medical Fellowship File 59, 2016. *Gender Dysphoria,* p. 2-3. Downloadable from www.cmf.org.uk

gender incongruence as a disorder, but rather, on the distress associated with it.

Approaches to treatment have also changed. Any attempt to try to "correct" a person's gender identity so that it conforms to their biological sex is now increasingly seen as unacceptable. It is now the body rather than the mind that is often treated, with hormones or surgery being used to change the body so it conforms to a person's sense of identity.

Some voices have been raised to question the appropriateness of these changes in medical approach. For example, a group of American pae- diatricians have recently spoken out against the practice of providing puberty-suspending hormonal treatment for children who believe they are the opposite sex.[14] Their statement uses strong language:

> *Young children are being permanently steri- lised and surgically maimed under the guise of treating a condition that would otherwise resolve in over 80% of them. This is criminal.[15]*

The paediatricians point out the damage that would be caused if other cases where there is incongruity

---

14 This treatment has been available in the UK on the National Health Service (NHS) since 2014.

15 www.acpeds.org/normalizing-gender-dysphoria-is-danger- ous-and-unethical

between a patient's mental and physical state, such as anorexia, were treated in the same way. Surgery to "affirm" the patient's false assumption that they are overweight, perhaps by liposuction, might reduce their emotional distress, but it will not have addressed the underlying psychological problem and will result in significant physical harm, even death.

Dr Paul McHugh, formerly Psychiatrist in Chief at Johns Hopkins Hospital, uses the same argument against sex-change surgery for adults. His hospital had pioneered the procedure, but then stopped offering it once evidence suggested that, although most of those who had received it were "satisfied" with the results, their psychosocial adjustments were no better than for those who hadn't. He writes,

> *I concluded that to provide a surgical altera-*
> *tion to the body of these unfortunate people*
> *was to collaborate with a mental disorder*
> *rather than to treat it.*[16]

Those who speak against the current consensus in this way can expect a backlash and are likely to be accused of the latest thought crime: "transpho-

---

16 www.firstthings.com/article/2004/11/surgical-sex
  Studies of the outcomes for those who have received sex-re-assignment surgery published since he wrote that article have not led him to change his mind. See Lawrence Mayer and Paul McHugh, p. 108-113

bia". This term is often extended to include not just those who fear or mistreat transgender people but anyone who doesn't fully support the idea of gender fluidity. A recent guide to transphobic hate crime defines transphobia as "intolerance of gender diversity ... based around the idea that there are only two sexes—male or female, which you stay in from birth".[17] Even Germaine Greer, an icon of the feminist movement, was accused of transphobia when she publicly declared her view that a transgender person who has gone through male-to-female surgery isn't really female, but is still a man with a different kind of body. As a result she was banned from various student meetings around the UK.

How do we explain the extreme reaction against those who dare to raise their heads above the parapet and question any aspect of the new transgender consensus? The answer is surely that this debate goes far deeper than scientific and medical arguments. It involves a clash of worldviews. We may have rejected the concept of objective truth as a culture, but we still expect everyone to hold to certain fundamental convictions—and one of them is the absolute right of each individual to define themselves as they wish. Any perceived challenge to that right is regarded as heresy and is strongly resisted, no matter what it's based on.

---

17 James, p. 3, quoting a transphobia fact sheet from Gallup.

Behind the different points of view are not only different worldviews but different gospels: different understandings of what leads to freedom and fulfilment. The "gospel" story which the world tells us goes something like this:

> *For years our spirits have been suffocated by restrictive traditions and morality. But now we must have the courage to follow our own light. We must resist anyone or anything that stands in our way. We must discover the hero inside ourselves and enter into the freedom that comes when we become who we really are.*[18]

What does Christianity have to say in response to this? Sadly, so often all we've been heard to say is the repetition of a set of laws—"Do this!" "Don't do that!"—which sound like the very opposite of good news. But, as we'll see in the next three chapters, the Bible tells a different story of oppression, liberation and freedom—a true story. But in the Bible's story, we are not the hero; God is. But, wonderfully, as we find our place within his story, we can discover our real identity, as well as true freedom and lasting fulfilment.

---

18 Based on a passage in Glynn Harrison, *A Better Story: God, Sex and Human Flourishing*, (IVP, London).

CREATION

CHAPTER THREE

In the beginning God created the heavens and the earth. Genesis 1 v 1

So God created mankind in his own image, in the image of God he created them; male and female he created them. Genesis 1 v 27

Creation is where the Bible story begins, and it is where our thinking about transgender must begin.

The Bible tells us that we did not emerge, by accident, from the cosmic soup. It states clearly that we've been created by a loving God. That means that we human beings are creatures, not machines—and that has a huge impact on how we think about our liberty.

True freedom, according to Scripture, is found not in asserting our radical independence and trying to be who we're not made to be. True freedom is found in embracing and *being who we are*. A fish that decides to make a bid for freedom by jumping out of the water will not be free—because it is created to live in the environment of water. And as soon as we try and become what we are not, far from enjoying freedom, we can't expect to flourish.

This conviction—that we're creatures, not machines—has massive implications. John Wyatt, in his book *Matters of Life and Death*, talks about a "Lego kit"[19] view of the human body. If we have just emerged from the primeval slime by chance, then there is no design whatsoever in how we happen to be. We are simply a collection of constituent parts that can be changed and adapted as we like. You can try to improve and upgrade to a different model—you can reprogram the machine because that's what we are. The structure of the body is value free, so if you want to change your sex, that's fine. If you want to make yourself bionic, that's fine too. In the words of the old Lego advert, "The only limitation is your own imagination".[20]

ART RESTORATION

John Wyatt contrasts that with what he calls the "art restoration view",[21] because, in the Christian

---

19 John Wyatt, *Matters of Life and Death*, (Nottingham: IVP, 2009, 2nd Edition), p. 35.

20 Wyatt, p. 35

21 Wyatt, p. 97-100

worldview, we are not machines—we are flawed masterpieces. We'll come to the "flawed" part later, but do you see the difference? If you see a work of art and you're asked to restore it, you don't look at it and say, "Well, I think he would look much nicer with a pair of spectacles". Or, "This scene would look better with a car instead of a hay cart". To do that is to break the code of the art restorer.

Art restorers respect the work, and know that their job is to bring out the artist's original intention. They work at cleaning and restoring the vivid colours. They study the work and the painter so that they can carefully get it back to what it once was. They work so that people can see the original in all its glory.

Humanity too is the work of an artist—a divine artist. Humankind is God's masterpiece—the pinnacle of his work of creation. Genesis tells us that when he looked at the people he had made, he declared them "very good". So identity is not for us to create. It sounds very freeing to say, "You can become who you want to be". But our *actual* identity, in that way of thinking, is completely invented, and therefore fluid, and therefore profoundly unstable.

It's no wonder that our culture, and many individuals within it, suffer from an identity crisis. Perhaps that explains the profound insecurity and anxiety of many young people. When I was at school, the biggest decision I had to make was what subjects to choose for my exams. Now teenagers are having to consider how to define their sexuality and gender.

An insecure identity may also be behind the growing trend for visiting speakers to be "de-platformed" by Student Unions. The extreme sensitivity of some groups, and the determination of others to protect them from hearing anything that might offend them, does suggest a deep insecurity. The resulting threat to free speech has caused widespread concern.

But the Bible brings great news to our culture with its identity crisis. And great news for people who are trying to work out who they are. It's wonderfully freeing to know that we live in a world made by a loving God, where identity is not something we've somehow got to create for ourselves. Our identity is a given. We're human beings, made in the image of God; we are creatures, not machines.

WHAT ARE WE?

As God's creatures we are not simply souls trapped in human bodies. He made us as physical beings; we are *embodied* creatures.

The ancient Greeks had a very low view of the body. The *psyche*, the soul, was the real you, but the body would just be discarded at death and then you'd go to the spirit realm. So in much Greek thinking, salvation was all about the freeing of the soul from the body that dragged it down. Our culture has largely returned to that mindset.

Caitlin, formerly Bruce, Jenner tweeted after she came out:

> *I'm so happy, after such a long struggle, to be living my true self.*

Caitlin was expressing this way of thinking: my feelings are my true self, my *psyche*. But in the Bible's understanding, because God created *everything*, the body and the whole material world is very, very good. Our bodies are an essential part of our true selves. So what I feel about myself can never be the whole picture, because God made us embodied souls. Our bodies are essential in determining and revealing who we truly are.

A low view of the body infected Christianity from the very beginning. Such thinking led some false teachers to urge believers to live an ascetic life, denying themselves physical pleasures, such as sex in marriage and the enjoyment of food. The apostle Paul strongly resisted them, insisting that "everything God created is good" (1 Timothy 4 v 4). All that he has created should be "received with thanksgiving" (1 Timothy 4 v 3). And that includes our bodies.

There were some in the church at Corinth who seemed to argue that it didn't matter that some believers were having sex with prostitutes. Sex just involved their bodies, but their souls weren't affected. But Paul is horrified by such thinking. He strongly opposes any dualism that divides the body and the soul: "The body … is not meant for sexual immorality, but for the Lord, and the Lord for the body … Do you not know that your bodies are temples of the Holy Spirit?" (1 Corinthians 6 v 13,16). That very high view of the body is rooted in creation. Matter matters because God made it.

So we should thank the Lord for our bodies. We should echo the words of the psalmist: "You created my inmost being; you knit me together in my mother's womb. I praise you because I am fearfully and wonderfully made" (Psalm 139 v 13-14). We should resist all the influences that lead so many to have a low body image and, rather than wishing we had been made differently, we should thank God for the body he has given us.

It's true, as we'll see in the next chapter, that our bodies have been affected by the fall. They are born with deformities and get sick. Accepting our bodies as gifts from God certainly doesn't mean that it's wrong to try and correct what's wrong with them and seek to bring healing. But as we do so, we should follow the "art restoration principle". The aim is to restore the Creator's intention; but we are not to try to change it. And that will certainly mean accepting the sex that he has given me.

WE ARE SEXUAL CREATURES

God made us *embodied* creatures and he also made us *sexual* creatures: "male and female he created them" (Genesis 1 v 21).

We're not just people who happen to have male or female genitalia. We are created men and women, and our sex, in the Bible's understanding, is fundamental to who we are.

We discover later in the Bible that the distinction between male and female is fundamental in contributing to a picture of the gospel and to the meaning and purpose of life. So we can't simply discredit it as the expression of some backward, ancient culture. The fact of the creation of human beings as male and female is woven deep into the fabric of the Bible's story, and therefore into the understanding of the world and ourselves that Christians embrace.

In Ephesians 5 the apostle Paul quotes the words of Genesis 2 v 24, which describe God's design for human marriage, with a man and a woman being joined together in "one flesh". He then writes:

> *This is a profound mystery—but I am talking about Christ and the church.* Ephesians 5 v 32

He is saying that the distinction between men and women reflects the distinction between God and human beings. And the coming together of a man and woman in the deep union of marriage is a reflection of God's desire for us to be united with him—which has now been made possible through Christ. Christ's church—those who trust in him—is his bride (Revelation 21 v 2). This picture only works because of the difference of the sexes. Two men or two women can't reflect the marriage of Christ and his church. The image requires the union of two distinct and different, but complementary, "others".

So, as God's creatures, we are embodied and sexual. And if we submit to the Creator, we're to accept our bodies and accept our biological sex as good gifts from him and seek to live accordingly. That view of who we are, stated at the very start of the Bible in Genesis 1 v 27, is quoted and affirmed by Jesus in Matthew 19 v 4.

That way of thinking, I take it, is the basis of the Bible's prohibition on cross-dressing:

> *A woman must not wear men's clothing, nor a man wear women's clothing, for the LORD your God detests anyone who does this.*
>
> Deuteronomy 22 v 5

WHAT THE BIBLE DOESN'T SAY

It's worth saying at this point that we should beware of pushing the Bible further than it goes. What you *don't* find in the Bible are lots of rigid rules about *what it means* to be a man and *what it means* to be a woman.

Often cultures will develop inflexible social codes that limit what is deemed to be masculine or feminine. But these go way beyond what the Bible says, and can lead to real tension and difficulty for those who don't quite fit those patterns.

So the boy who loves dolls and prefers ballet to football may be branded as "gay" or "girly". And the girl who prefers Action Man to Barbie and likes to climb trees is labelled a tomboy. Scripture nowhere gives a clear, narrow set of rules as to what a man or woman should be like, or a boy or girl.

So let's not forget that, yes, there *are* fundamental differences between men and women, but there are also many differences between men and men, and women and women. We're not to push the Bible beyond where it goes. But the basic message of creation is this: each person's biologically-determined sex is a good gift of God's creation. We should accept it and live within it.

One friend of mine, Sam Allberry, summed it up in these two tweets:

> *Our culture says: Your psychology is your sexual identity—let your body be conformed to it.*

> *The Bible says: Your body is your sexual identity—let your mind be conformed to it.*

A proper understanding of creation has to be the first building block if we are to understand the Christian perspective on transgender. But the next perspective will help us understand where we are today more clearly. Let's turn to the fall.

FALL

CHAPTER FOUR

We read about the next stage in the Bible's story in Genesis Chapter 3.

Now the snake was more crafty than any of the wild animals the LORD God had made. He said to the woman, "Did God really say, 'You must not eat from any tree in the garden'?" The woman said to the snake, "We may eat fruit from the trees in the garden, but God did say, 'You must not eat fruit from the tree that is in the middle of the garden, and you must not touch it, or you will die.'"

"You will not certainly die," the snake said to the woman. "For God knows that when you eat from it your eyes will be opened, and you will be like God, knowing good and evil."

> *When the woman saw that the fruit of the tree was good for food and pleasing to the eye, and also desirable for gaining wisdom, she took some and ate it. She also gave some to her husband, who was with her, and he ate it. Then the eyes of both of them were opened, and they realised that they were naked; so they sewed fig leaves together and made coverings for themselves.* Genesis 3 v 1-7

These well-known words are filled with profound meaning. The first humans were given great freedom: to enjoy and eat from every tree (Genesis 2 v 16), but with just one small prohibition, which was given for their protection. They were told not to eat of the fruit of the tree of the knowledge of good and evil (Genesis 2 v 17). The tree represents the fact that God alone has the authority to define what is good and what is evil, what is right and what is wrong. And by taking that fruit, human beings are saying, *No! We're not accepting that God alone is God. We're going to take that authority for ourselves. We are going to decide what is right and what is wrong.*

Satan, who appears in the story as a snake, tempts the man and woman with the promise that they can be like God. And what is it to be like God? It is to set the rules, to be in charge, to decide what is right and wrong. They believed the poisoned promise of the serpent—with disastrous results, not just for themselves, but for all their descendants and for the whole world.

Sin has now infected humanity, so all of us by nature follow in the way of Adam and Eve, in rebellion against God. And, because human beings were set over God's world, it was, in some mysterious way, bound up with them. We might see a parallel in the relationship between a nation and its leader—if the leader is corrupt, everyone is affected (as we've seen, for example, in Zimbabwe under President Mugabe). And so when human beings turned from God, this had consequences for the rest of creation. Because God will not let humans live in his paradise without him on the throne, the material world, including our bodies, has been spoilt. God's originally perfect creation is no longer as it was designed to be. The act of eating the fruit was a bid for "freedom" but it didn't deliver what Satan promised. Far from raising us up so that we are like God, our rebellion against him drags us down. We have fallen and are all affected. All of us are broken. All of us are disordered.

The Bible's insight that we are all both created and broken is vital for understanding not just transgender questions but every kind of human affliction—physical or psychological. We have all been profoundly impacted by the fall.

DISORDERED BODIES

The fall affects us all physically in many different ways. Our bodies get sick and decline as we get older. It's a depressing thought that we reach our physical peak in our early twenties—and then it's downhill all the way after that! Some of us were born with deformities, and that includes those with intersex conditions.

Up to about 1% of people are born with conditions in which their chromosomes or their sexual or reproductive anatomy does not fit what is typical for men or women. These include, for example, Klinefelter syndrome, which affects up to 1 in 500 men who have two or more X chromosomes, and hypospadias, a malformation of the penis, affecting up to 1 in 250 men. The 1% figure is sometimes used to argue that it is inappropriate to speak of biological sex in binary terms. But it must be stressed that the sex of almost all that 1%, including those with Klinefelter syndrome and hypospadias and a number of other conditions in this category, is not in doubt.

The term "intersex" is often therefore reserved for those whose sex at birth is ambiguous, so that it is very difficult, or impossible, to identify their sex simply by looking at their genitalia. This is very rare indeed, affecting only about 1 in every 5,000 births (0.02%).[22] They have been affected by disorders of sexual differentiation in the developing embryo and should not be regarded as a "third sex".

In these situations doctors and parents may have to make difficult decisions as to which gender they are going to assign the child at birth. Best practice seems to be to keep corrective surgery to a minimum in infancy and to raise the child according to its genetic sex. That gives time to see what impact hormones have at puberty and to allow individuals to make their own decisions as they mature. In such cases it is entirely appropriate that some kind of medical intervention may later alter the person's sex from what was assigned at birth. This physical condition is clearly in a completely different category to gender dysphoria, which stems from the mind, emotions and sense of identity.

DISORDERED MINDS

But it is not just our bodies that are affected by the fall. All of us are affected psychologically by the fall to some extent or other. We struggle, for example, with stress, anxiety or depression. A Christian worldview encourages humility and compassion towards others, because we don't view some people as broken, and others as

22 Sharon James, p. 5

unbroken. We understand that we are *all* affected by the fall, but in different ways.

All of us experience some form of alienation. Perhaps, for example, we don't feel we fit in socially with those around us or we're not happy with our body shape. Those who experience gender dysphoria feel alienation from their biological identity as men or women. We have seen already that there is no agreement on what causes this, and it is likely that causation varies from person to person. In very general terms we can say that it is the result of sin— as is everything that spoils life on earth. If human beings hadn't turned from God, everything would still be perfect. But it's very important that we don't move from the general to the specific and imply that an individual's gender dysphoria is because of their own personal sin. It may be that there are some genetic influences involved in some cases. And when experiences in childhood are contributing factors, they may well involve an individual being sinned against by others. Walt Heyer, for example, a man who for many years thought he was really a woman, has written of the damage caused to him by his grandmother, who frequently encouraged him to wear a chiffon dress when he was a boy.[23]

---

23 *I was a Transgender Woman* by Walt Heyer. Heyer transitioned to life as a woman and had sex-change surgery before later identify-

Those of us who experience same-sex attraction may see parallels at this point.[24] We didn't simply choose to be attracted to the same sex; causation is much more complex than that. So we shouldn't feel guilty or ashamed about it. The same is true for all of us in a fallen world. We may well not be responsible for the particular struggles and temptations we have, but we are, of course, responsible for how we respond to them.

We have disordered bodies. We have disordered minds. But there is more...

DISORDERED HEARTS

The greatest and perhaps the most significant effect of the fall on all of us is that we have disordered hearts. The apostle Paul speaks in Romans 1 of how human beings turn away from their Creator and worship instead created things, and the result is, he says, that...

> *their thinking became futile and their foolish hearts were darkened.* Romans 1 v 21

The problem is not just that we sin—that we break

---

ing once more as a man. www.thepublicdiscourse.com

24 I have written about my same sex attraction in an interview in *Evangelicals Now*: "A battle I face". www.e-n.org.uk/2012/10/features/a-battle-i-face/

God's law. It's that we *want* to sin. The problem is within; it's in our desires. We have disordered hearts.

One of the ways in which the sinful folly of our minds and hearts is seen is that we turn away from what is natural to what is unnatural. Paul's repetition of the word "exchange" is striking. Sinful humanity "*exchanged* the glory of the immortal God for images" (v 23). "They *exchanged* the truth about God for a lie" (v 25). And that suppression of God's truth was then worked out in their behaviour: "Even their women *exchanged* natural sexual relations for unnatural ones. In the same way the men also abandoned natural relations with women and were inflamed with lust for one another (v 26-27).

When Paul describes behaviour that results from rebellion against God, he does not begin with homosexuality because he thinks it is the worst sin—worse, for example, than murder, which appears as part of a longer list a few verses later. The Bible is certainly not obsessed with homosexuality—in fact it's only explicitly mentioned in three passages in the New Testament.[25] He presumably mentions it here because it is a clear example of the point he is making. Perverse thinking (the exchange of the worship of God for the worship of things he

---

25 Romans 1 v 26-27; 1 Corinthians 6 v 9-10;
    1 Timothy 1 v 9-10.

created) leads to perverse behaviour (for example, the exchange of natural relations for unnatural ones). We show our rebellion against God in a particularly obvious way when we refuse to go along with the way in which he has made the world, such as in the division of the sexes.

That certainly doesn't mean that those who go against the natural order God has created by acting on a desire to have sex with people of the same sex, or by rejecting the sex they were born with, are more sinful than anyone else. Those sins are particular examples of the natural tendency of all sinful humanity to turn away from our Creator and his will for our lives. None of us should look down on anyone else. Just a few verses later Paul writes, "You ... have no excuse, you who pass judgement on someone else" (Romans 2 v 1). And at the conclusion of this section of his argument he stresses that, "there is no one righteous, not even one" (3 v 10). We all have disordered hearts.

So as we think about those who struggle with transgender issues (or as we wrestle with them ourselves) we will see them differently as we look at them with the biblical perspectives of creation and fall in our minds. We will never give in to a "yuk" reaction, because they are beautiful and precious creatures made in God's image. But neither will we give way to the false notion that "they were made that way". We are *created* but *fallen*. We are *made* but *marred*. And those who experience gender dysphoria, along with all of us, are both victims of the fall, and therefore to be sympathised with, and also, to some degree, sinners with disordered hearts who need to be both forgiven and rescued.

And it is to that rescue we turn now...

RESCUE

CHAPTER FIVE

We saw in chapter two that the iWorld encourages us to see our lives as a story in which I am the hero. The real, authentic me has been suppressed and cramped by external forces, such as religion, society and traditional morality. So it's up to me to rescue myself: to assert my own individuality and be true to myself.

But, as we've seen in the last two chapters, the Bible tells a very different story. We don't have to create ourselves; God has already done that. But, by turning away from him, we have spoilt everything. It's true that religion, society and traditional morality can be oppressive, but they're not the fundamental problem. The fundamental problem is sin—human rebellion against God, which has spoilt the whole created order, including ourselves. Where once there was perfect harmony, now there is disorder. And we can't sort that out, because we're part of the problem. We need a hero other than ourselves.

Wonderfully, God in his grace sent his Son, the Lord Jesus Christ, to be that hero. He is the rescuer we so desperately need.

THE PERFECT HUMAN

The rescue begins with Christ being born on earth as a human being. That is a wonderful affirmation of our created bodies. The Son of God was born in human flesh! And he wasn't a generic—a character-less template of a human being. He was born, raised and lived as a man.

And what a life he lived! He was so different from Adam, the first man. Adam was not content just to be human. He wanted to be like God. But, far from rising, he fell and dragged all humanity down with him. But Christ, although he was "in very nature God … made himself nothing … being made in human likeness" (Philippians 2 v 6-7). And he did it for us.

Adam wasn't God, but he tried to become God. Jesus was God, and remains fully God, but he didn't cling to all his privileges. He became a man and then, in his earthly life, lived as Adam should have lived—as we should have lived, in perfect submission to his heavenly Father.

His perfect obedience was seen supremely in his death: "even death on a cross" (Philippians 2 v 8). Because he never sinned, Jesus didn't deserve what Adam and Eve experienced and what all humanity experiences by nature—separation from God. But on the cross he willingly stood in our place, representing sinful humanity as he died. He took our separation from God upon himself so we needn't face it, if we trust in him.

And then, wonderfully, Jesus rose again. His bodily resurrection is another massive affirmation of the importance of our bodies. It's a very clear statement that God is committed to the material world. He is committed to rescuing not just our souls but our bodies too and the whole created order. The resurrection is a foretaste of what is to come when God will redeem the whole creation and establish "a new heaven and a new earth" (Revelation 21 v 1).

That new creation awaits the second coming of Christ at the end of time. In the meantime the good news about salvation through Christ is to be preached throughout the world. Those who turn from their rebellion against God and trust in him are given a new identity. The most common description of Christians in the New Testament is as those who are "in Christ". We have been profoundly connected to him by the Holy Spirit. That means that God sees us as those who are joined with him. We have died with him. In God's sight our sins have been paid for already. And, spiritually speaking, we have been raised with Christ. We are no longer separated from God, but rather, enjoy a new life in fellowship with him, our heavenly Father. And one day, after his return, we'll be physically raised with him.

We will always be insecure if our identity is based on something within us: our feelings, assertions or achievements. But this new identity in Christ that he offers us could not be more secure. We will often fail God, but our relationship with him remains unshakeable because it is founded not on anything we do but on what Christ has already done for us. Through all the ups and downs of life we can be absolutely sure of God's love. He is not just our Creator but our Redeemer as well.

This new identity is offered to everyone equally. There is no hierarchy within God's family, as if some are closer to him than others because of their race, social rank or sex. That is Paul's point in Galatians 3 when he writes,

> *So in Christ Jesus you are all children of God through faith … There is neither Jew nor Gentile, neither slave nor free, nor is there male and female, for you are all one in Christ Jesus.*
> Galatians 3 v 26, 28

These words should not be taken out of context to imply that the differences between the sexes have been obliterated by Christ.

THE CHRISTIAN EXPERIENCE NOW

While we wait for the new creation at the return of Christ, we still live in a fallen world and continue to experience the pull of sin in our lives. But, wonderfully, we are no longer enslaved to it. We have been set free from the penalty of sin because of Christ's death for us. And we are being set free from the power of sin by the work of the Holy Spirit within us.

By the Spirit we have been given new hearts, so that our deepest desire is now to love and please God. As Paul puts it, our "minds are set on what the Spirit desires" (Romans 8 v 5). But our old sinful desires also remain, so there is a tug of war going on between them and the new desires God has given us by the Spirit: "The flesh desires what is contrary to the Spirit, and the Spirit what is contrary to the flesh. They are in conflict with each other" (Galatians 5 v 17). The way of holiness is to "keep in step with the Spirit" (5 v 25), resisting sin and living according to God's will.

The modern idea is that we have to affirm the feelings we have and that we can only be authentic as we fulfil our desires. But the Bible teaches that some of our desires should be resisted. We are to measure our desires and feelings against the will of God, as the Spirit through the Bible makes us sensitive to those things that grieve him, and helps us to want to live in ways that please God.

The way in which God works to grow us in Christian maturity is rarely by removing the obstacles of our disordered bodies and minds. Very often, God allows them to continue. And amazingly, through the ongoing struggle with our disordered bodies and minds God renews the inner person, so that we become more and more like Christ. It seems to me that some of the great heroes of our faith are those who go on with very deep struggles. Some of them are bodily—a profound disability perhaps. Others are psychological—depression perhaps, or ongoing gender dysphoria. But as Christians determine to walk the way of the Spirit and to praise their Creator, their faith grows and deepens, and they become more and more like Jesus.

For someone who struggles with gender dysphoria and becomes a Christian, there is no promise that those feelings will go away. But they have been promised the presence of the Holy Spirit, who assures them of their new identity as God's children, and gives them a new longing to please him. That will involve recognising that what ultimately matters is not what my feelings may say about myself, but who God made me to be, which is who I will be in the resurrection. My origin and destiny in Christ should therefore affect how I live now. And that origin and destiny includes my body, with its sex.

That means that those who experience gender dysphoria should resist feelings that encourage them to see themselves as anything other than the sex of their birth. They will sometimes fail, whether in thought or deed, as we all do, but they are called to persevere. That may feel agonising at times—as if they are putting themselves to death. But that is the way of life to which Christ calls all of us. The cost will become very real for us in different ways, given the different challenges we face, but we are all summoned to deny ourselves, take up our cross and follow Christ (Mark 8 v 34). There is pain in that—sometimes very great pain. But when we kill the desires that lead away from God's will, it brings life, not death. Paul writes,

> *We who are alive are always being given over to death for Jesus' sake, so that his life may also be revealed in our mortal body.*
> 2 Corinthians 4 v 11

He is talking about the wonderful way in which God is at work in us as we deny ourselves in following Christ. He is with us every step of the way. Even in

great hardships we can know deep joy and content-
ment from knowing his love. And, as we gradually
grow in the likeness of Christ, we become more and
more the people we were meant to be.

The gospel offers forgiveness, a fresh start in life, a
new strength for genuine change, and a new family
to belong to. It is a message for everyone—including
those who struggle with all kinds of questions about
their identity. Jesus said:

> *Come to me, all you who are weary and
> burdened, and I will give you rest.*
>
> Matthew 11 v 28

Christians want to make the same invitation to
people today. We don't say to people, "Get yourself
fixed and then come to Jesus". That's not how it
works. We say to people, "Come to Jesus and he
will start to put you together again". And that is
the experience of being a follower of Jesus now. We
are all works in progress in some way or another.
No one who follows Jesus has cause for pride in
anything other than the Saviour who paid the price
to set them free.

In the midst of joy, the pain for Christians of
living in a fallen world will continue. If anything,
it is intensified by what we have already received in
Christ. We are like the child who has been allowed
to lick a spoon to get a taste of the delicious dessert

that has just been cooked, but must then wait until the meal to get a full portion. We have already received a taste of the wonderful salvation in Christ and we long for more. As those who have received "the firstfruits of the Spirit", we "groan inwardly" as we wait for the fullness of salvation when Christ returns (Romans 8 v 23). And one day the waiting will be over.

THE NEW CREATION

There is a final chapter in the history of the world and our lives.

Although we will continue to struggle in all kinds of ways, it will not go on for ever. When Jesus Christ returns and we are raised to be with him, we will have perfectly restored bodies and perfectly restored minds, in a perfectly restored world. All our struggles will be over. There'll be no more crying or mourning or pain (Revelation 21 v 4). No more psychological alienation, but a wonderful sense of being at one with who we're meant to be—men and women perfectly restored into the image of God, together praising and glorifying him.

There is a sense in which we are all looking for peace and rest. We are hungry for these things because we have been made for them. In the new creation we will enjoy rest from the struggles that we all have because of the fall. And we will enjoy the peace and harmony that the first man and woman had in Eden. This is the Christian hope—a hope that we can be confident in because Jesus has paved the way through his suffering on the cross and his resurrection from the dead.

WISDOM

CHAPTER SIX

You might be thinking, "Well I understand some of this, but how does this outline of the big story of the world apply in the very specific circumstances of my life? How does it apply specifically to the gender questions I have, or to friends or relatives?"

Applying these truths to complex questions requires us to exercise wisdom. And the aim of this short book is to give us the tools to start to think and talk biblically—not necessarily to answer all our questions. Here are a few pointers to get us started.

1. HOW SHOULD WE RESPOND PERSONALLY?

Maybe you are facing these struggles yourself. I hope that yours is not a lonely battle. I would say that about any of the struggles we face in life. Please don't let it be a lonely battle and especially don't let shame keep it a lonely battle. We're not meant to fight alone. We're meant to fight within the family of God.

If you're a Christian facing this battle, can I also say that this struggle, these feelings, *do not define you*? They may, at least partly, describe *how* you are, but they do not describe *who* you are. If we are Christians, our identity is as men and women in Christ; and our goal, by the Holy Spirit, is to seek to align our desires and our behaviours to our new identity in Christ. We're not to allow our old desires to define our identity and dictate our behaviour. Rather, we must allow Jesus Christ by his Spirit to give us our identity as sons and daughters of God. And then the Holy Spirit will help us to conform our desires and our behaviour to that identity. That will take a lot of effort and challenge. It will demand careful thought and persistent prayer, and you won't be able to do it on your own.

2. HOW SHOULD A CHURCH RESPOND?

It's wonderful when you read the Gospels to see that the Lord Jesus Christ welcomed absolutely everybody. Maybe you're reading this book, and you think, for whatever reason, "Because of the kinds of things I feel and think or the kinds of things I've done, Christ would never welcome me."

If this describes you, can I urge you to simply read the Gospels, and see how Jesus treated broken and sinful people like you and me. He really did welcome *everyone*. He welcomed the misfits and the outcasts and the people who the self-righteous religious establishment dismissed and had nothing to do with. Jesus loved them and welcomed them.

And when we move on to the book of Acts, we find, as far as we can tell, that the first Gentile (non-Jew) who became a Christian was an Ethiopian eunuch—someone who, in today's language, might be described as gender queer.

So I hope very much that church families will follow the example of Jesus and show a warm, non-judging welcome to everyone. I was visiting one church, and saw someone arrive who was very obviously transgender. I thought to myself "How are they going to respond?" I wondered if they might turn away or show disgust, or just stare. But no—no one batted an eyelid. They greeted the individual with a smile and a kind word, just as they did for everyone else. And I thought, "What a lovely thing that is". Giving a warm welcome should be our first instinct.

If we meet someone who's not a Christian, and is transgender in some kind of way, and they come to church, our great longing for them, above all else, is that they'll come to know the Lord Jesus Christ. In order for them to know his love, we need to *exhibit* that love. And that certainly means that we should never be making jokes, either from the front in meetings, or in private conversations, about transgender issues or people.

And if someone with gender dysphoria is a Christian, let's not expect instant Christian maturity from them. It's often as people are welcomed within a church family that they'll begin to understand a bit more what the Bible teaches and what that might look like in practice in their own life. The issues are complex, especially for those who have already transitioned and may have had surgery. We will hope that a Christian will want to accept their biological sex and live accordingly, but what that will look like may vary from person to person. And change will certainly not happen overnight, so we need to be patient in caring for one another and instructing one another. Some of our struggles are more obvious than others, but all of us are works in progress. So we need to support and encourage each other as we try and grow together into the likeness of Christ.

3. WHAT SHOULD I DO IF MY CHILD TALKS ABOUT HAVING TRANSGENDER FEELINGS?

Don't panic.

If your child doesn't always act in the stereotypically "normal" way for a child of their sex, this needn't be a cause for alarm. Remember that, yes, there are differences between men and women. But there are also huge differences between men and men and between women and women.

Don't assume, just because your child doesn't always do what you think most boys or most girls do, that there's a great problem and you need to panic about it, or seek professional help. Parents need to be wary of overly-rigid stereotypes because that can actually cause problems in itself.

But don't dismiss it either. Discussion needs to be encouraged, and we should resist the temptation to hide our heads in the sand and hope it all goes away.

Parents also need to be active in teaching children the goodness of God and the gospel of grace. Show them how the Bible makes better sense of the world than the other ideas they come across. Model for them what it is like to live as forgiven sinners who are wrestling with our fallenness as we look towards the new creation.

Although for most children, so research shows, these feelings will disappear as they reach adolescence, for some they will continue, and they will need a robust Christian worldview to face life.

4. WHAT IF A CLOSE FAMILY MEMBER OR FRIEND CONFIDES IN US?

It may be that they are either thinking of transitioning or they've already decided. How might we respond?

I hope that the first response with those we love very much and we know well will be to love them and to affirm our love for them and then to listen. There has already been a huge journey for them to arrive at this conclusion, and the first thing we need to do is listen and understand. It will be with considerable pain and fear that they have "come out" to you—so you need to recognise this and thank them for being honest with you. We could ask further questions like: How did you come to that point? What's it been like for you? What things have you particularly struggled with?

Very likely they will have a huge fear of rejection and they will need you to express your love for them, and your affirmation and understanding of them as a person with these feelings. I would suggest that, only then—in the context of an ongoing, loving friendship—will we be in a position to gain a hearing for what the Bible teaches. We will perhaps need to explain why we can't endorse a particular course of action that they are planning to take. But we can only do this helpfully if it's in the context of a loving and supportive relationship.

5. WHAT ABOUT THOSE LESS CLOSE TO US?

Perhaps you have an acquaintance—maybe someone who studies or works with you or who lives nearby—who you know to be transgender in some way. How you react will very much depend on the nature of the relationship. If it's someone we know more closely, we might say something; if it's someone we don't really know, why would we make any comment to them? Because transgender issues can present in such an obvious way, we might be tempted to put them into some kind of "special category". But in reality, they are just like you, me and anyone else: broken sinners in need of God's love and forgiveness.

In speaking with transgender people, love, wisdom and respect are the watchwords and, in my opinion, respect will mean calling someone by the name they choose to be called by. It's going to be very hard to establish a relationship with someone if we won't use the name they have chosen. And then, depending on the relationship, over time we might have an opportunity to sensitively share the good news and explain our own convictions.

6. HOW DO WE RESPOND TO OUR CULTURE?

There are big issues in our culture that can be worrying for Christians. Now that the transgender agenda has been brought under equality laws, there are concerns about all kinds of things. It is absolutely right that transgender people should be protected from injustice. For example, the law should certainly intervene if a transgender person is refused admission to a public place, like a shop or restaurant. But should a church which doesn't think it is right for someone to transition from their biological sex be allowed not to consider a transgender person for employment? What about the right to be saying what I'm saying in this book? Some protections have been secured in the existing legislation, but how long will they last?

These are valid concerns and we should be supporting groups who are engaged at the cultural and political level in order to win a hearing for Christian voices among lawmakers and to protect the right of Christians to hold our convictions and live by them. We need to support them.

And we should be prepared to speak up ourselves in support of the goodness of God's creation of human beings as men and women. The distinction between the sexes is increasingly being undermined, especially in schools, where the concept of gender fluidity is often promoted. Christian parents and governors will surely want to express concern when this happens.

But the most important thing that our culture needs to hear is the gospel of Jesus Christ. They need to hear that the "freedom" offered by individualism is not a freedom at all. It has left people feeling very, very lost. If we've just emerged by chance, there is no answer to the question "Who am I?". I don't know who I am. I've got no identity beyond what I have made up for myself. I'm lost. And I'm lonely too, because if I'm being encouraged to push my own agenda and create my own individual identity, then inevitably we're going to clash with one another, and that will drive us apart.

As we have seen, the Bible gives a very, very different view. It speaks of a God who made us and loves us—a God who has rescued us and given us a glorious future. It tells us we're not alone in the universe. We're not lost. We don't desperately have to try and discover who we are and fight for who we are— it's a wonderful given. Sadly, the identity that we've been given at creation has been flawed and broken because of our sin, but God has committed to putting it right and we can live today as part of a wonderful story. Jesus the rescuer has come already. He has died, he has risen, he has sent his Spirit and made possible the transformation that we all need as broken people. We are broken physically, broken psychologically, broken in our hearts—but if we have trusted in Christ, God has begun that transformation in us which will continue until completion, when at last we'll be put back together—body and soul perfectly integrated for the glory of God.

FURTHER READING

For a recent authoritative review of the scientific research on transgender, see *Sexuality and Gender. Findings from the Biological, Psychological and Social Sciences.* Available from www.thenewatlantis.com

Mark Yarhouse, *Understanding Gender Dysphoria* (IVP Academic, 2015)

Sharon James, *Are we all "omnigender" now?* Article in The Bulletin by Affinity. Download at www.affinity.org.uk

Christian Medical Fellowship *File 59 2016 Gender Dysphoria*. Download from www.cmf.org.uk

Al Mohler, *We Cannot Be Silent: Speaking truth to a culture redefining sex, marriage, and the very meaning of right and wrong* (Thomas Nelson, 2015)

For a more general book on sexual identity in young people, see Mark Yarhouse, *Understanding Sexual Identity* (Zondervan, 2013)

ACKNOWLEDGEMENTS

I am grateful to Rob and Claire Smith, Tim Keller, Sam Allberry, Ed Shaw, Matthew Mason, Clare Heath-Whyte and Tamar Pollard for reading the manuscript and making some very helpful comments. Tim Thornborough has done a superb job as editor and Luke Cornelius has helped me enormously through his typing, perceptive observations and much else besides.

the good book
COMPANY
Opening up the Bible

At The Good Book Company, we are dedicated to helping Christians and local churches grow. We believe that God's growth process always starts with hearing clearly what He has said to us through His timeless word—the Bible.

Ever since we opened our doors in 1991, we have been striving to produce resources that honour God in the way the Bible is used. We have grown to become an international provider of user-friendly resources to the Christian community, with believers of all backgrounds and denominations using our Bible studies, books, evangelistic resources, DVD-based courses and training events.

We want to equip ordinary Christians to live for Christ day by day, and churches to grow in their knowledge of God, their love for one another, and the effectiveness of their outreach.

Call us for a discussion of your needs or visit one of our local websites for more information on the resources and services we provide.

UK & EUROPE
NORTH AMERICA
AUSTRALIA
NEW ZEALAND

thegoodbook.co.uk
thegoodbook.com
thegoodbook.com.au
thegoodbook.co.nz

0333 123 0880
866 244 2165
(02) 6100 4211
(+64) 3 343 2463

WWW.CHRISTIANITYEXPLORED.ORG
Our partner site is a great place for those exploring the Christian faith, with a clear explanation of the good news, powerful testimonies and answers to difficult questions.